Original title:
Juniper Journeys

Copyright © 2025 Creative Arts Management OÜ
All rights reserved.

Author: Christian Leclair
ISBN HARDBACK: 978-1-80566-771-1
ISBN PAPERBACK: 978-1-80566-841-1

## The Solace Found in Solitude

In a world of quirky gems,
I sit alone with my pens.
A sock puppet joins the play,
Telling secrets night and day.

The fridge holds my closest friends,
With yogurt that never ends.
I share my thoughts with all the cheese,
It listens while I sip my teas.

My cat, the judge, gives me a stare,
As I dance around without a care.
The vacuum mocks my moves with glee,
We laugh together, just us three.

In solitude, I've found delight,
With mismatched socks and candlelight.
Each whimsy dance, a joyful shout,
Who would've thought? I'm never out!

## Canvases of Wild Dreams

Once I painted skies of green,
And wrestled with a grapefruit queen.
My canvas laughed at colors bold,
As brush strokes whispered tales untold.

A ladder climbed to reach the sun,
And paint splatters turned to fun.
A rainbow dance across my floor,
With jellybeans that I adore.

My muse, a squirrel with a flair,
Gave me tips beyond compare.
He said, "Go wild, let colors clash,
Just make sure you avoid the trash!"

In my world of vibrant schemes,
I find my joy in wild dreams.
With every stroke, a giggle blooms,
Creating art in zany rooms.

## **Whispers of the Evergreen**

In the woods where whispers play,
Trees wear hats of green all day.
Squirrels gossip, oh so spry,
While birds just laugh and aim for the sky.

A raccoon in shades looks quite the sight,
Dances at the moon, a true delight.
With every twirl, he wags his tail,
Even the trees start to turn pale!

## Underneath the Sky of Boughs

Underneath branches, a picnic laid,
Ants soon join, a bustling parade.
One grabbed a chip, oh what a thief,
While the others cheer, 'Get the beef!'

A sandwich fight? You'd better bet!
Birds throwing crumbs like a fun duet.
Laughter echoes through the green,
As squirrels roll past in a wacky scene.

## The Path of Aromatic Shadows

A path of scents, a fragrant tease,
Where pinecones giggle in the breeze.
Something smells sweet, oh what a treat,
But it's just a skunk dancing on his feet!

With every step, a giggle erupts,
The shadows wobble, nature interrupts.
Who knew that walking could be so fun?
With every twist, there's laughter spun!

## Echoes in the Forest Mist

In the fog, the trees play tag,
Chasing reflections that seem to brag.
A toad croaks out a silly tune,
That makes the mushrooms sway 'neath the moon.

Echoes bounce like rubber balls,
Frogs leap up; nobody falls.
With each hop, the laughter grows,
In a forest full of jokes and pros!

## **Blades of Grass and Sighing Winds**

In the meadow, blades so keen,
A tickling dance, quite serene.
The grass whispers jokes to the breeze,
While ants do the cha-cha with ease.

Laughter floats on the summer air,
A butterfly laughs without a care.
The sun winks down, a playful spark,
As squirrels plot mischief in the park.

Bees buzz by, cracking wise,
While sunflowers gossip, oh so sly.
A rabbit hops in, wearing shades,
Making grand entrances in green glades.

With every gust, a new prank to unfold,
Grass tickling toes, yet never gets old.
Nature's own comedy, a wondrous show,
Where laughter reigns, and good vibes flow.

## **Patterns of a Starlit Canopy**

Under the vast, twinkling dome,
Stars play hide and seek, far from home.
A comet rushes by with flair,
While owls debate who's got the best hair.

The moon grins down, a cheeky sight,
With craters that look like acne bites.
Fireflies flash, a disco ball glow,
Inviting all to join in the show.

Long shadows stretch, a playful tease,
As raccoons plan a mischief spree.
Each twinkling star shares a cosmic pun,
In the night's embrace, all the fun begun.

Galaxies giggle, asteroids roll,
Laughter echoes into the night's stroll.
As patterns weave, dreams take flight,
Under this canopy, all feels right.

## Echoes of the Elder Grove

In the grove where the old trees speak,
Whispers of wisdom, and laughter they tweak.
The trunks are wise, yet full of cheer,
As birds drop jokes for all to hear.

Beneath their boughs, the shadows play,
Squirrels retell yarns in their own way.
Roots dig deep with tales of yore,
While critters join in, craving more.

With the rustling leaves, laughter stirs,
Echoes of giggles in nature's purrs.
Branches sway like dancers old,
In the grand performance, where fun unfolds.

Logs tell tales of a silly past,
Where nothing's serious, and joy's amassed.
Under the watchful gaze of time,
Life blooms with laughter, simply sublime.

## Ramblings in the Quiet Glade

In the glade, where silence dreams,
A chipmunk snickers at sunbeam schemes.
The daisies gossip, their heads held high,
While mushrooms eavesdrop, sly as a spy.

Softly the breezes tease the leaves,
Tickling branches, the laughter weaves.
The earthworms wiggle, their dance so grand,
While snails take shortcuts—life's not so planned.

In the still of the shade, a soft thrum,
Nature's song, an amusing hum.
A frog croaks rap, with rhythm divine,
While crickets strum on the vine.

As dusk creeps in with a wink and grin,
The glade giggles, revealing kin.
In this haven, fun is the creed,
Nature chuckles, fulfilling every need.

## **Visions Cradled in Orchard Shade**

In the orchard, shadows dance,
With squirrels in their silly prance.
Apples giggle on the trees,
Whispering jokes in the warm breeze.

Nature's laughter fills the air,
Bees buzz by without a care.
The branches bend with playful grace,
As fruits try on a sunny face.

A wise old owl takes a peek,
As ripe peaches start to speak.
Every critter wears a smile,
While we sit back and stay awhile.

Beneath the shade, we share our cheer,
With strawberries lending an ear.
Together in this fruity space,
Life unfolds at a funny pace.

## A Serenade to Quiet Wonders


A toad sings softly by the creek,
In croaks that tickle, not a squeak.
The daisies sway, a charming sight,
While fireflies twinkle, what a night!

A raccoon winks with mischief's glee,
As he steals snacks from under a tree.
The moon peeks down with playful eyes,
While crickets chirp their lullabies.

The breeze hums tunes of secret dreams,
Where laughter bubbles, or so it seems.
In this woodland, magic's not far,
Just look for giggles where you are.

A serenade to nature's jest,
Each quiet wonder, a cheerful guest.
The woods, our stage, with no regrets,
In every nook, joy subtly begets.

## The Alchemy of Light and Shade

A sunbeam slipped through leafy green,
And found a bug in the in-between.
Together they plotted quite a show,
With antics that made the flowers glow.

A shadow danced on the forest floor,
While owls winked from wisdom's door.
The sunlight giggled, a playful tease,
As leaves sang softly in the breeze.

Mice in hats join the grand parade,
While mushrooms join them, unafraid.
The world turns bright in this game of light,
As shadows stumble, embracing delight.

The alchemy of shade and sun,
Turns ordinary into funny fun.
In this kaleidoscope, laughter plays,
Transforming the mundane in so many ways.

## Tangled Threads of Nature's Quilt

In nature's quilt, each thread is spun,
With wildflowers weaving in the sun.
A bumblebee hums a silly tune,
As daisies nod beneath the moon.

Spider silk glistens with morning's dew,
A giggling web hosting a view.
Frogs in their croaks form a band,
While butterflies float, so charming and grand.

The trees exchange whispered secrets bold,
With stories of mischief still retold.
Each patch of earth as silly as can be,
In a landscape buzzing with glee.

Tangled threads in this vibrant lore,
Create a tapestry where laughter soars.
From roots to tips, let the joys unspool,
In this playful paradise, nature's school.

## A Dance with the Twilight Mists

In twilight's grip, we prance, oh dear,
Each misty gust brings giggles near.
We twirl and leap, no care in sight,
A dance with shadows, what a delight!

With friends like these, how can one frown?
We trip on roots, we tumble down.
The moon's our spotlight, a radiant glow,
As laughter echoes through the woe!

## The Lullaby of the Nightingale

A nightingale sings, but off-key,
Each note a joke, oh can't you see?
The stars snicker in the velvet sky,
While the crickets laugh, oh my, oh my!

She tries to woo a lady fair,
With silly tunes, we can't help stare.
A serenade, or was it a jest?
The woodland critters sure know best!

## **Storms Among the Tall Pines**

Amid the pines, the winds do whip,
With gusts that make my sandwich skip.
A tree trunk laughs, it bends and sways,
As raindrops join our silly play!

But lightning strikes, oh what a fright!
The squirrels scream and take to flight.
A storm of giggles, nature's tease,
As chaos reigns among the trees!

## The Lament of the Wandering Breeze

Oh, wandering breeze, what tales you weave,
Whisking away the leaves, I grieve.
You tickle noses, make hair fly,
Yet sigh with sorrow as you pass by.

A whisper here, a chuckle there,
You play with hearts without a care.
But catch you not, you dance away,
Leaving us here in disarray!

## Nature's Threads in the Treetops

In branches high, a squirrel scampers,
It thinks it's sly, but sees my cameras.
The robin sings, a raspy tune,
While chasing bugs beneath the moon.

Down below, the ants parade,
With tiny hats, their grand charade.
They march and dance, a fancy sight,
In nature's ball, they prove their might.

A raccoon sneaks with mischief planned,
His paws all smeared in peanut butter sand.
His jig is quick, he trips and falls,
Off dusty rocks, he tumbles small.

Above the scene, the laughter swells,
In these green woods, where humor dwells.
Nature's threads weave tales so bold,
In playful hues and laughter gold.

## Odyssey of the Earthbound Soul

A turtle strolls upon the path,
With every step, he draws a laugh.
His heavy shell, a built-in chair,
He stops for snacks, without a care.

A fox runs fast with socks askew,
He jumps and twirls in a lively view.
His antics wild, a comic dance,
An uninvited, furry prance.

The deer perform a graceful leap,
Yet trip and tumble, their form so cheap.
They giggle softly as they rise,
In nature's playground, joy never dies.

The earthbound souls in playful game,
With every mishap, they're never lame.
For laughter's path, they boldly chase,
In this grand adventure, they find their place.

## Whispers of the Evergreen

The pines gossip in the breeze,
They tell tall tales with utmost ease.
A woodpecker drums a silly beat,
While squirrels giggle, quick on their feet.

The flowers bloom with colors bright,
They wink at bees in pure delight.
A ladybug launches, grabs a ride,
It's not so tough, they laugh and glide.

A rainbow lizard does a twist,
Entwined with laughter that can't be missed.
He jumps from leaf to leaf with flair,
Waving hello this way and there.

In whispering woods, the fun abounds,
With chuckles echoing all around.
Nature's humor, a joyous spell,
In the evergreen, all creatures dwell.

## The Path of Hidden Shadows

Through shadows long, the creatures creep,
While cricket choirs lulled us to sleep.
A bat with glasses zooms too fast,
In midnight antics, he'll never last.

A hedgehog rolls with spiky charm,
Yet stumbles hard in a grassy farm.
He shakes it off with a playful grin,
Saying, 'I'll laugh; let the fun begin!'

A rabbit hops with floppy ears,
Squeezing through ferns that bump his fears.
He's a comedian in the moonlit shroud,
As shadows dance, he's well-endowed.

The path goes winding; the laughter flows,
In hidden nooks where the chortle grows.
Nature's stage, where humor's found,
In hidden shadows, joy's renowned.

## Etchings on the Bark

Scribbles in wood, oh what a sight,
A raccoon reads poems by the moonlight.
Squirrels debate on the latest craze,
Enjoying their nutty dialogue plays.

Bark covered stories, tales of a fright,
Of chipmunks who dance each and every night.
The owl hoots loudly, a comedic tune,
As laughter spills out under a laughing moon.

Nature's mischief in every groove,
The trees tell secrets that make us move.
So join in the fun, don't let it slip,
Leave your own mark on this woody trip.

## Labor of the Wandering Heart

The wanderer trips on roots and moss,
Chasing after dreams, but oh what a loss!
His compass goes wild, spins like a top,
Leading him straight to a berry shop.

He thought of grand lands and faraway trails,
But settled for snacks and some fishy tales.
A squirrel throws peanuts, a mock cheer squad,
While the wanderer winks, feeling quite odd.

"Adventure's afoot!" he shouts with great glee,
But his feet are stuck under a laughing tree.
With giggles and snacks, who cares where to roam?
Home is the laughter, the heart, and the foam.

## Beneath the Gnarled Yew

In shadows of branches that twist and twine,
A hapless beetle looks for a sign.
He thinks he's a knight, in a grand metal suit,
But really he's lost on a big green root.

The yew chuckles low, in the afternoon sun,
As ants march in cadence, thinking it fun.
A ladybug laughs at the knight's mighty fight,
"Next time, dear beetle, try flying in flight!"

They gather for stories, as day fades to night,
With tales of the breeze, they laugh in delight.
So beneath gnarled branches and whispered old lore,
Nature's comedy thrives, begging encore.

## Serene Retreats Under Growing Canopies

In a spot where the sunlight plays peek-a-boo,
A turtle reclines like a laid-back guru.
He chuckles at crickets who sing off-key,
While mocking the dance of a bumbling bee.

Amidst the green shades where misfits convene,
The squirrel holds court, wearing a crown of green.
He gestures with acorns, declaring their might,
While the others join in for a nutty good night.

So raise up your glasses, and shout with delight,
In this canopy world where the critters unite.
Each moment is precious, with laughter and cheer,
Together they thrive in this whimsical sphere.

## Beneath the Denim Sky

Under denim skies, we danced with glee,
In hats too big, we felt so free.
With squirrels in tow, we pranced around,
In our mismatched socks, we lost our ground.

Sipped lemonade with a twist of lime,
We laughed at jokes that stood the test of time.
A parade of ants on a crumbly ride,
While the moonlit laughter became our guide.

We spun in circles till we lost all sense,
Trading silly stories, just pure nonsense.
With laughter echoing through the starry night,
In our wonderful world, everything felt right.

So, beneath the denim sky so wide,
We took a leap, and joy became our guide.
With every hiccup and snort of bliss,
We found our happiness in moments like this.

## Tales from the Gnarled Roots

From gnarled roots, stories arise,
Of squirrels with dreams and cheeky spies.
A chipmunk's heist of acorn gold,
Turns into legends that never get old.

With each twist and turn in the forest's tale,
We hear the whispers of owls that sail.
They chuckle at secrets of clumsy deer,
And spread the news of mischief far and near.

Beneath the shady branches so wide,
We crack up at misfits who've got no pride.
A raccoon wearing a bowl on his head,
Claims it's a crown, but we're all misled.

As night falls softly on our tangled roots,
We dream up more tales in our crazy boots.
Each laugh and snicker lifts us up high,
In the land of the stories, we never say die.

## **Wandering Through Fragrant Evergreens**

Wandering paths where the evergreens grow,
With sniffly noses and hearts all aglow.
Bumping into trees that just love to tease,
We'd giggle and tumble, falling with ease.

A little fox joined in for some fun,
Chasing our shadows, he said, "Let's run!"
Through fragrant pines, we laughed 'til we cried,
With every wild turn, our worries just died.

We stumbled on mushrooms that danced in the mist,
Each step brought more joys we couldn't resist.
As squirrels cheered us on with a jump and a shout,
We vowed to return, without any doubt.

So here's to the laughter and trees standing tall,
In a world made of giggles where we're having a ball.
With every adventure beneath nature's sheen,
We find our wild dreams in the evergreen scene.

## **Secrets of the Mountain Breeze**

The mountain breeze carried secrets so light,
Tickling our ears with a playful delight.
Whispers of stones and the birds' silly tunes,
Dancing with laughter beneath the full moons.

We climbed up high with sandwiches packed,
Each bite dripped mustard; we didn't look back.
With clouds for pillows and stars for our beds,
We put on our hats and lifted our heads.

The breeze told tales of a goat with a hat,
Who wore it with swagger, and that was that.
We chuckled aloud at his quirky charm,
With every gust, we felt nature's warm arm.

So let's chase the giggles, let worries all cease,
In the arms of the mountains, we find our peace.
Through whispers and chuckles, we wander with ease,
Exploring the world in the mountain breeze.

## The Wildflowers' Secret Confessions

In the meadow, flowers chat,
Telling tales of their petal hat.
They argue who wears a better hue,
And giggle about the bees they pursue.

Dandelions puff, but never shy,
They whisper secrets to the sky.
They mock the roses' thorny plight,
Saying, "Our fluff's just pure delight!"

Violets boast of their sweet perfume,
While daisies dance upon the bloom.
They've got a wildflower code, you see,
To laugh and play, just wild and free.

With every breeze, they sway and tease,
Creating laughs from the rustling leaves.
In their patch, life is quite absurd,
Who knew flowers could be so heard?

## **Dreamscapes of the Woodland**

In the woodlands where mushrooms grow,
A squirrel juggles acorns to and fro.
Frogs croak in tune with the songbirds' croon,
While owls pretend to snooze by the moon.

The rabbits host a dancing spree,
With quirky steps and giggles of glee.
Each twirl is met with a stampede,
Of grasshoppers joining in the deed.

Chatty chipmunks, full of sass,
Throw nutty jokes and never pass.
They turn the trees to a laugh parade,
In their world, no such thing as shade.

When night falls, they wear glittery capes,
As the foxes waltz with funny shapes.
Under the stars, they twinkle bright,
Dreamscapes made of pure delight.

## Threads of Time in the Willow's Weave

The willow tree tells tales so old,
Of playful breezes and leaves of gold.
It sways and laughs, a sight to see,
Whispering secrets, just you and me.

Ladybugs race up and down its bark,
While fireflies flicker, igniting the dark.
Time bends here, moments intertwine,
Each giggle captured like dew on a vine.

A woodpecker drums a silly beat,
As squirrels tease with acorns to greet.
The threads of time, they twist and twirl,
In the willow's weave, life's a merry whirl.

Nature's fibers, woven with care,
With laughter and joy floating in the air.
From dusk till dawn, the stories flow,
In the willow's embrace, we laugh and grow.

## Nature's Palette Under Twilight

When twilight falls, colors collide,
The sky paints laughter, a vibrant ride.
Crickets chirp in a cheerful tune,
While moonbeams giggle, floating like balloons.

The colors dazzle, greens into blues,
As butterflies gossip sharing their views.
They twirl around blooms, oh what a sight,
Creating art in the fading light.

A badger trips on a tuft of grass,
With a snort and a grunt, he tumbles past.
Nature chuckles, a misstep or two,
In this palette, there's room for the new.

As night deepens, sparkles emerge,
Stars wink at the critters, a cosmic urge.
In every stroke, there's playful grace,
Nature's canvas, a merry place.

## The Serenity of Solitary Trails

On paths where shadows play,
I trip on roots that sway.
My hat flies off in glee,
The trees just laugh at me.

With each misstep I make,
I hear the branches shake.
A squirrel chases my shoe,
While I just mumble, 'Phew!'

The calm is like a joke,
As I dodge the sneaky oak.
I dance with the wild grass,
And hope no one will pass.

Nature's giggles abound,
Where awkwardness is found.
In my own little show,
I'm the star—don't you know?

## Whispered Wishes in the Greenery

In the bushes, whispers soar,
Like wishes at a store.
I asked for luck today,
But found my shoe in clay.

The ferns conspire and tease,
While I trip over bees.
A butterfly takes flight,
I wave, then lose my sight!

Amidst the playful leaves,
I find my heart believes.
A secret path appears,
I follow—grinning ears!

With giggles in the air,
And nature's wild flair,
Each wish gets tangled tight,
In this whimsical night.

## Light Filtering Through Emerald Leaves

Sunbeams dance through the boughs,
I admire nature's brows.
But when I go to snap,
A branch gives me a tap!

The light makes shadows play,
While I yell, 'No way!'
A moment's blissful peace,
Until I lose my lease.

The leaves sparkle and glow,
And then I see a crow.
He laughs at my surprise,
I just roll my eyes.

As I trip down the lane,
My joy ignites the rain.
A sunbeam starts to tease,
In these emerald trees.

## Awakened Spirits in the Foliage

In foliage thick and bright,
Spirits giggle at my plight.
I wander off the track,
With a fungal snack on my back!

"A twist and turn," they sigh,
As I reach for the sky.
I tumble through the ferns,
With every laugh that burns!

The owls roll their big eyes,
As I plot my next surprise.
A toad hops with delight,
Saying, "Stay there, that's right!"

In this wild romp I roam,
Each blunder feels like home.
The spirits are my friends,
With humor that transcends.

## The Whispered Promises of Pines

In a forest where whispers lie,
The pines conspire, oh my, oh my!
They giggle and sway, in the breeze so free,
Leaving secrets for squirrels, just wait and see.

The critters all dance, in marvelous glee,
As wisps of green share their jests, can't you see?
The branches, they chuckle, with ticks and tocks,
As raccoons in tutus do calisthenics on rocks.

The sun peeks in with a glint of surprise,
Tickling the needles, and oh, how they rise!
With laughter resounding, they sway side to side,
While woodpeckers join for a laugh-filled ride.

Nature's roundtable, no fuss and no fight,
With every tall tale told, they revel all night.
So heed when you wander, through scent and through sound,
For in pine-scented air, joy's always around.

## Verses from the Wilds

In the wild, where the odd things creep,
Frogs wear top hats, taking a leap.
A hedgehog recites lines full of flair,
While the rabbits in bow ties do style their hair.

The owls play chess, with mushrooms as pieces,
While raccoons throw parties, and laughter increases.
The trees twist their limbs, join in on the fun,
As fireflies wink, saying, 'Party's begun!'

Beneath the bright stars, the whippoorwill sings,
An anthem of joy, of nature's mad flings.
The flowers wear crowns, in a colorful spree,
As the bees serve the drinks, oh can't you see?

With critters all gathered, no worries in sight,
They rally round tales till the dawn brings its light.
So if you feel lost in your own jumbled roads,
Just follow the laughter where wildness explodes.

## An Odyssey Through Verdant Valleys

Through valleys so green, where the wild things bloom,
A ferret with glasses reads tales from a room.
While turtles in vests stride with pride and panache,
Each step is a journey, with giggles and crash.

In meadows, the daisies compete for some fame,
Claiming titles like 'Funniest Flower' in the game.
While bees buzz with jokes, that they quickly refine,
True comedy gold, straight from the divine.

The brook joins in too, with a babble of wit,
As frogs pull their antics, all ready to flit.
An otter rolls over, chatters in streams,
Bringing forth laughter, as bright as our dreams.

So wander through valleys, let merriment reign,
Where every small creature has something to gain.
With smiles and with chuckles, take heart in the play,
For joy is a journey that leads you our way.

## The Aroma of Earth After Rain

When raindrops retreat, leaving scents in the air,
The mud does a jig, with a twist and a flare.
Worms in tuxedos perform fits of delight,
As beetles in bowler hats dance through the night.

A puddle reflects, with a wink and a grin,
The antics of ants that are ready to spin.
They march in a line, with a purpose so grand,
Clutching little umbrellas in their six tiny hands.

The smell of the wet earth, a fragrance so bright,
Invites even rain clouds to join in the light.
While gophers crack jokes from their plush, cozy dens,
And raccoons on stilts share their newest trends.

With laughter a' mingling, past hearts that all frown,
The earth's merry fragrance unites every town.
So when the rains fall, and you feel drained of cheer,
Just sniff out the giggles - they're always right here!

## Rituals of the Forest Beneath

Under the roots, the squirrels dance,
Twisting their tails in a comical prance.
Mushrooms gossip, the ferns they sway,
In a woodland ball where they laugh and play.

Pinecones chuckle, sharing their tales,
Of critters in stoles, wearing tiny scales.
The brook giggles, bubbling with glee,
As frogs serenade with a croaky spree.

The owls hoot riddles, wise and absurd,
While fireflies flicker, the night vision blurred.
A raccoon juggles acorns with flair,
In the heart of the forest, nothing's too rare.

So gather 'round, in the moonlight's glow,
Where the trees hold secrets few ever know.
Join in the laughter, let worries depart,
For the humor of nature is a true work of art.

## Conversations with Skylarks

Skylarks talk nonsense, flapping their wings,
Debating the merits of imaginary things.
One claims he found a cloud made of cheese,
While the other just chuckles, soaring with ease.

They gossip of humans, so clumsy on ground,
Whom they imitate, flapping round and round.
"Look at that fellow, thinks he's a bird!"
As they burst into laughter, it's truly absurd.

They sing of the sun and the moon's funny fight,
How they argue over who brings more light.
With each silly note, they tickle our ears,
Turning our worries to giggles and cheers.

So listen in closely, let joy take its flight,
In the airy realms where the skylarks delight.
For the world's full of wonders, so offbeat and bright,
In the conversations that lift us to new height.

# The Vision of Autumn's Embrace

In autumn's glow, leaves twirl like dancers,
Each step they take, the ground entrances.
A squirrel in sunglasses, munching on pie,
Winks at a crow who just flies on by.

Pumpkins are giggling, they're rolling downhill,
"Watch where you're going!" they squeak with a thrill.
Corn stalks play tag, swaying left and right,
In this festival realm, there's no end in sight.

The harvest moon chuckles, why's it so round?
Reminds the scarecrow of his floppy old ground.
With cackles and gales, they tumble through air,
In this whimsical world, forget every care.

So as colors shift, and the days fade away,
Join in the laughter, come out and play.
With autumn's embrace wrapped snugly around,
Find joy in the quirky, where fun can be found.

# Legends Carried by the Winds

The winds whisper legends of silly old trees,
Who debated the clouds and the buzzing of bees.
One claimed he'd seen rainbows slide down the trunk,
While the others just giggled, calling him bunk.

From pine to oak, the stories they weave,
Of a snail who believed he could gallop and leave.
Each gust that blows shares tall tales anew,
Of a duck who once thought he was a kangaroo.

They dance with the dandelions, twirling their fluff,
Telling grand tales about being quite tough.
With every breeze bringing laughter galore,
The legends unfold, forever and more.

So listen now closely to the tales of the air,
For laughter and legends are woven with care.
The winds carry secrets, of witticisms grand,
In this playful domain, let your spirit expand.

## A Hike Through the Sapphire Woods


In sapphire woods, where squirrels prance,
  I tripped on roots, missed my chance.
    A deer in shades of twilight blue,
      Laughed at me, as if it knew.

A bird sang tunes, off-key and bright,
  I asked for help, it took to flight.
The trees looked down, so tall and grand,
  Whispered secrets, didn't understand.

With every step, my shoes would squeak,
  The path was winding, not for the meek.
    I met a fox with shoes like mine,
    We danced around, how divine!

    At last I found a picnic place,
      Cupcakes hidden, not a trace.
Gobbling crumbs with all my might,
  The squirrels cheered—what a sight!

## Cradle of the Wild

In wild cradles where creatures roam,
I lost my way, far from home.
A raccoon winked, a bit too spry,
With snacks in paws, it caught my eye.

The trees swayed low, said 'Join the fun!'
But I was busy, chasing sun.
A bear split berries, what a treat,
He offered me a seat, oh sweet.

With giggles spilled on mossy beds,
We shared wild tales and toasted breads.
The grass was soft, the laughter loud,
As nature wrapped us in her shroud.

When dusk approached, the fireflies danced,
I waved goodbye, the raccoons pranced.
With fond memories tucked away tight,
I promised to return one night.

## The Blue Needles' Embrace

In blue needle pines, I found a friend,
A squirrel who told jokes with no end.
He said, 'If you trip, just laugh it off!'
And with that, he made me scoff.

We rolled down hills, amidst the clover,
Hoping our wild antics would not be over.
The trees stood tall, like guardians wise,
But giggles erupted, in surprise.

A pine cone flew, caught in mid-air,
And landed softly, without a care.
We crowned a mushroom, a king of the lot,
Declared a feast, on the forest pot.

With bows and cheers, the day did fade,
In the blue needles' embrace, memories laid.
I bid adieu to my furry mate,
As twilight beckoned, it couldn't wait.

## Echoes of the Forest Heart

In echoes deep, the forest chortles,
Where every critter plays in portals.
A bear with shades and ice cream cone,
Slipped on a branch, and fell like stone.

The trees chuckled, a hearty laugh,
As I tried to take a witty photograph.
But my camera flashed, it scared the deer,
Who darted away, oh dear, oh dear!

A raccoon offered me some fries,
With saucy grins and mischievous eyes.
We partied hard till stars gleamed bright,
In echoes of the forest heart, pure delight.

I danced with shadows, twirled with glee,
As the moon peeked in, just to see.
With every giggle, the night grew bold,
Stories spun in whispers, forever told.

## Realm of the Pine Cones

In the kingdom of pine cones, so round and so wise,
Each one is a ruler with secrets and ties.
They chuckle and whisper, oh what tales to unfold,
Of squirrels in royal coats, brave and bold.

The ground is their throne, so soft and so green,
They wiggle and giggle, a sight to be seen.
With hats made of needles, they dance with delight,
Chasing the shadows, retreating from light.

## The Gentle Call of Distant Hills

The hills called my name with a voice like a breeze,
Inviting my feet to skip, jump, and tease.
I tumbled and fumbled, tripped over a rock,
Yet laughter erupted; what a silly shock!

The daisies all nodded, they giggled with glee,
As I spun in a circle, oh so carefree.
With a skip and a hop, I made quite the scene,
As bumblebees buzzed, and the sun painted green.

## The Language of Leaves and Stones

Leaves rustle and whisper secrets of old,
While stones sit and ponder, their wisdom yet bold.
I asked, 'Oh dear leaves, what's the catch of the day?'
They twirled on their branches, 'Come dance, come and play!'

The stones sighed and chuckled, 'We prefer to be still,
But your dancing is quite the extraordinary thrill!'
They winked at each other, with a grin on their face,
While I stumbled around, trying to keep pace.

## Footfalls Through the Untamed

Through thickets and brambles, my feet go astray,
Each footfall is a giggle, come join in the fray.
With branches that slap me, I leap and I bound,
Each step is a riddle where laughter is found.

A deer passed me by with a cheeky little glance,
As I waltzed with the wind in a clumsying dance.
The wildflowers chuckled, they joined in the fun,
In the untamed wilds, I felt like the sun!

## **Wandering Through Needle-Laden Trails**

In the woods where shadows play,
Needles prick without delay.
I trip on roots and say a string,
Oh, nature, you are quite the king!

Squirrels laugh, they hide and tease,
Chasing me up through the trees.
With a nut in hand, they laugh away,
I wonder who's the fool today!

Berries bubble, colors bright,
I thought I'd pick, but what a fright!
Turns out they're just a mean old prank,
Now my tongue's a vibrant tank!

I tumble down a fuzzy hill,
Ouch! My rear, I feel the chill.
But laughter echoes in the air,
Adventure waits for those who dare!

## In the Company of Wild Roots

Roots are my pals, they pull me low,
I'm dancing now, but moving slow.
They giggle as they trip my feet,
Who knew that mud could taste so sweet?

With vines like snakes, I'm caught in glee,
"Join us, friend!" they laugh at me.
Listen close, they have their say,
"Can't catch a break, no way, no way!"

Feeling spry, I sway and twirl,
Then faceplant into a leafy swirl.
All the roots, they cheer and clap,
I'm a star, but what a mishap!

Among the greens, I roll and bound,
Who knew laughter could be so profound?
With silly friends, I can't complain,
Let's dance again through growth and gain!

## Starlit Songs of the Pines

Under stars, the pines do sway,
They croon and hum a tune today.
I join in with my off-key song,
The trees agree: I can't go wrong!

An owl coos, "What's that you croak?"
I giggle back, "Just a little joke!"
The forest giggles, whispers loud,
As I dance amidst the crowd.

With twinkling stars, we form a ring,
Pine cones flying—oh, the zing!
I dodge and weave, I laugh and dive,
In this wildness, I come alive!

As morning peeks with golden rays,
I'm still here, to the pines, I praise.
For every note, for every cheer,
This silly song I'll always hear!

## The Dance of Wandering Winds

Oh windy friend, come dance with me,
Twirl around, feel wild and free.
You whip my hair and spin my dress,
I tumble down—oh, what a mess!

Through valleys deep and hills so high,
Together we will surely fly.
The trees look on with winking eyes,
They cheer us on as we arise!

Whisked away, my laughter flies,
In gusts that swirl beneath the skies.
A tumbleweed rolls by my side,
"Let's have some fun!" it seems to chide.

We race the clouds, we chase the sun,
What a silly, wild run!
With every giggle, every cheer,
The dance of winds brings joy so near!

## Mystical Trails and Twinkling Stars

In the forest, I took a stroll,
Tripped on roots, oh what a toll!
Squirrels giggled, pointing in jest,
"You're the clumsiest soul, that's the test!"

Moonlight danced with a cheeky grin,
Stars above did a spin and spin.
A raccoon laughed, wearing a hat,
"You should join my circus, what of that?"

Paths that twist like a noodle's curve,
Every twist makes my tummy swerve.
I chased a shadow, it led me astray,
"Hey! Come back! You can't run away!"

With a squeak and a shout, I did complain,
Nature's quirks drive me half insane!
But with each laugh in the moonlit glade,
I cherish the fun, it won't soon fade.

## Where the Moss Grows Soft

Where the soft moss grows in the shade,
I found a frog in a tiny parade.
With a top hat made of a leaf so grand,
He croaked out tunes, oh wasn't it planned!

Nearby a snail, quite slow and sage,
Wrote a novel but lost the page.
"Who needs speed? I'm a thinker!" he said,
As he pondered the world from his mossy bed.

A squirrel zoomed by with snacks on his back,
"You slowpokes need to pick up the slack!"
But we all just laughed as he tripped on a twig,
Turns out, even fast ones can play the big jig!

In this green realm, where giggles abide,
Life's petty troubles can easily slide.
Together we chuckle, in laughter we thrive,
Where the moss grows soft, we feel so alive!

## Dreaming Beneath the Canopy

Beneath the canopy, I lay down,
Listening to nature's silliness sound.
A floppy-eared bunny hopped on my chest,
"Wake up, sleepyhead! You're missing the fest!"

The trees were gossiping, oh what a show,
Telling secrets that only they know.
A wise old owl, perched high with flair,
Said, "It's a drama—we're all in despair!"

With giggles and whispers, the forest alive,
My dreams took flight, making me dive.
A flying fish challenged me to a race,
Who knew "tree-diving" was such a wild place?

So here in the shade, with laughter my guide,
I belly-flop into the dreamlike tide.
Under swaying branches, I joyfully find,
The magic of silliness, oh so unconfined!

## The Spirit of the Sagebrush


In the land of sagebrush, winds do swirl,
A tumbleweed danced with a twirl.
I chased it as if it were my lost shoe,
But it laughed and said, "Catch me if you do!"

Cacti sported hats of sunshine bright,
Quipped, "Join us, young lad, for a cactus fight!"
But I'd rather sip from the clear, cool stream,
Than join prickly pokes in their silly scheme.

The lizards did gossip, all green and spry,
"Did you see that fellow try to fly?"
Laughter echoed through sandy trails,
As I stumbled upon tales that never fail.

With each chuckle shared in the golden glow,
The spirit of sagebrush, oh how it flows!
A riot of humor in every soft breeze,
In this desert of dreams, I'm blissfully pleased.

## The Call of the Wooded Realm

In the forest, squirrels plot,
Leaves whisper secrets, often forgot.
Rabbits dance in mismatched shoes,
Wits fly as high as the dragonflies' views.

A bear in a hat, what a sight,
Tripping on roots, he's in for a fright.
Trees chuckle softly as they sway,
Nature's comedy steals the day.

A hedgehog makes a fine ballet,
Pretending he's slick, but rolls away.
With pine cones as props, they play their roles,
Laughter echoes through the woodland strolls.

Mice in tuxedos throw a feast,
While owls critique as their guests, to say the least.
Join the fun, don't miss the show,
In the wooded realm, there's laughter in tow.

## Folklore from the Thicket

Beneath the boughs, the legend blooms,
Of a frog who was king with threadbare looms.
He croaked his tales to a crowd of ants,
While fireflies twinkled their night-time rants.

A raccoon, a thief with a shiny knack,
Stole a pie, then wore a cape like a hack.
With a wink and a grin, he dashed from the scene,
His laughter rang out, a bandit so keen.

Wolves in the woods, with their silly tricks,
Playing charades with well-timed kicks.
"Who's afraid?" they whimper and tease,
In the thicket, fear's just a breeze.

The stories keep spinning, each funnier still,
Of animals plotting, of whimsy and thrill.
In the heart of the thicket, they gather to chat,
Sharing their fables, where nonsense is that.

## A Tapestry of Fragrant Memories

Each flower a story, each scent, a cheer,
Daffodils giggle while orchids jeer.
A rose named Rosie loves to sing,
While daisies dance, it's a parlor thing.

Lavender whispers her secrets so sweet,
While the thyme does a jig on his tiny feet.
Petunias chuckle at the gossip spread,
As marigolds all nod their heads.

In this patch of fragrance, mischief's afoot,
Sunflowers beam where humor is put.
With each breezy laugh, the petals swish,
Creating memories, oh what a wish!

As the day fades into a kaleidoscope hue,
The garden erupts, like a show just for you.
A tapestry woven with laughter and glee,
In each fragrant corner, we long to be free.

## Veins of Green Beneath Our Feet

Wander through vines, where giggles grow,
The grass hides secrets we all yearn to know.
With roots wrapping tales in a leafy embrace,
Let's dance on the soil, it's a curious race.

Snails with top hats, taking their time,
Gossiping moss gives a velvety rhyme.
Beetles rejoice in their gleaming parade,
And daisies clap hands, never afraid.

Underfoot, the whispers of ages gone past,
In the mushrooms' shade, we gather at last.
With laughter erupting like bubbles of cheer,
The veins of green pulse with whimsy so near.

Every stomp is a stomp on a tale yet untold,
Nature's jokes wrapped in emerald and gold.
So come take a stroll; let absurdity reign,
In this verdant kingdom, where silliness gains.

## The Enigma of the Fern Frond

In a garden full of chatter,
The ferns hold secrets, little and scattered.
One claims to dance with the breeze,
While another just giggles with ease.

A snail in a race, caught in green ties,
Challenged a ladybug, oh what a surprise!
But with a slow crawl, and a wink of an eye,
The fern said, 'They're both just too shy!'

Peeking from shadows, the ivy takes notes,
Of whispered plans that the wild thyme promotes.
A hedgehog believes he's the king of the weeds,
While daisies are plotting their flowerbed creeds.

Laughter echoes through petals that sway,
All believing they've much more to say.
In this realm of green, where jokes come alive,
Who knew that roots could be so sly?

## Fables of the Forest Floor

Underneath the leafy dome,
Lies a tale that's far from home.
A mushroom shouted, 'I'm the best!'
While ants had a party, truly a fest!

A wise old tree with a worried frown,
Said, 'These stories should never go down.'
But the acorns just rolled, giggling afloat,
Claiming they'd soon win an award for their quote!

A crow tried to sing, but just got it wrong,
"Caw, caw, caw-ny-way," was his froggy song.
The fox rolled on in, yawned with delight,
'In this barding tree, who will take flight?'

Mossy characters joined in the joke,
While spiders spun tales, wrapped up in smoke.
And in this curious, leafy parade,
Lies a forest full of memories made.

## Whispers of Weathered Wood

A plank of wood with tales to tell,
Whispers on breezes, a ticklish spell.
'Though I may creak, I've got style!'
Hums a board who's aged with a crooked smile.

The squirrels debate about nuts and their fate,
While a grumpy old tree counts the years, quite straight.
'Life's but a jest,' chuckles the pine,
'We all wear rings, like a curvy design!'

Bears pass by, trying hard not to laugh,
At the woodpecker's attempt to take a photograph.
But with a peck, that snapshot was surely vain,
As the tree moved, causing a bit of strain.

The age of this wood holds wisdom and fun,
In jesting echoes, where stories are spun.
Here laughter breaks through as each segment is stored,
In the heart of the wood, joy is adored.

## Hushed Secrets of the Clearing

In a bright open space, secrets conspire,
While butterflies gossip about dreams that inspire.
'What if the sun wore a silly hat?'
Wondered a flower, with a curious spat.

A rabbit hops in, with a spring in his step,
Holding a clipboard, taking his prep.
'Count the giggles and hops, oh my dear!
We'll throw a grand bash for all of us here!'

The chatter in petals quickly took flight,
Anticipating laughter that stretched into night.
Chirping crickets practiced their jokes wittily,
While frogs croaked a tune, oh so spiritedly.

As the moon cast its glow on the glade's silly forms,
And shadows danced lightly, forming quirky norms.
Here in this clearing, where laughter's the aim,
Every hush is a chuckle, in friendship's true name.

## Refreshing Breezes and Ancient Trees

In a forest where whispers roam,
A squirrel claimed a mighty dome.
He tried to fit, oh what a sight,
But got stuck, oh what a fright!

The wind laughed, a playful tease,
As he waved his tiny knees.
From branches high, the birds all sang,
While the squirrel just dangled and dang!

A breeze swirled round, a tickling cheer,
With nutty snacks drifting near.
He wriggled hard with all his might,
And flew off the branch—what a flight!

So remember the tales of this tree-bound friend,
Where laughter and mischief never end.
In forests full of quirky glee,
There's always a squirrel stuck in a tree!

## The Heartbeat of the Mountain Grove

In a grove where shadows dance,
A raccoon got caught in a prance.
He slipped on leaves, went for a spin,
Shouting, 'Who let the party begin?'

Under moonlight, the critters swayed,
But the raccoon was unafraid.
He twirled and twitched, his tail a whip,
And joined the owls for a wild trip!

The trees all chuckled, their branches swayed,
As rabbit beatboxed, a tune he played.
"Let's dance!" squeaked the little frog,
While the fox crooned into the fog.

And if you wander there one night,
You might just catch that silly sight.
In the grove where the funny beats grow,
Just watch out for raccoons on a show!

## Fables from Forested Heights

Once a moose tried to climb a stone,
Declared it his, but it wasn't his throne.
He slipped and flopped, a clumsy affair,
With chipmunks just gasping for air.

The trees chuckled, their laughter loud,
As the moose blushed, embarrassed and proud.
With grace not found, he strutted back down,
Imitating a king with an awkward crown.

A wise old owl hooted so sweet,
"Just be yourself, friend, admit defeat!"
The moose then laughed, a newfound cheer,
Bounding off—no more worries here!

So heed this tale from heights above,
Where laughter grows, and there's always love.
In forests where mischief takes flight,
Even moose can learn to dance with delight!

## Tales Woven with Twigs

Gather 'round for tales untold,
Where the branches twist and fold.
A hedgehog planned a grand parade,
But forgot those pesky twigs he'd made.

He rolled and pined, with an empty cart,
Chasing dreams with a heavy heart.
But soon he found a twiggy friend,
A mouse who brought his band to lend.

With drums made out of acorns tight,
They marched along, what a silly sight!
Singing songs about fuzzy feet,
While weaving in and out on repeat.

So join this twiggly, jiggly fun,
In a world where pranks are never done.
Where hedgehogs dream and mice all hum,
And laughter's a tune that never goes numb!

## Serendipity Beneath the Canopy

In the shade of leafy green,
Squirrels dance, a funny scene.
Chasing tails, they laugh and shout,
While birds gossip about their route.

A picnic lost, a sandwich flies,
Landing right before my eyes.
Who knew lunch would take a trip?
As bugs line up for a tasty sip!

With melons rolling, laughter loud,
We join the critters, feeling proud.
Between the trees, where shadows play,
Every misstep makes our day!

So here we sit, beneath the sun,
In nature's chaos, it's all in fun.
With every giggle, we understand,
Life is best in this wild land.

## Roots that Bind

These tangled roots have stories shared,
Of every critter that has dared.
The rabbits giggle, the badgers snort,
As they recall their woodland sport.

One fell flat, a muddy cheer,
The owls hooted, oh what a year!
A snail in style, with shells of bright,
Wanders slow but feels so right.

Each creature here, a nutty friend,
Their quirky tales never seem to end.
With furry antics, under the moon,
We laugh together, the perfect tune!

So here we share the roots we've sown,
In this odd place, we've truly grown.
Connected by laughter, wild and sweet,
These roots that bind are quite the treat!

## Mystic Teas of the Woodland

In a kettle, leaves collide,
A brew of mischief, come inside!
With mushrooms dancing, herbs that giggle,
Each sip brings forth a joyous wiggle.

Tea time here is quite absurd,
With laughs and tales just like a bird.
The raccoons host with such delight,
Under the stars, into the night.

A sprinkle of spice, a dash of cheer,
Each cup raises a quirky leer.
The forest drinks, it's quite the show,
While all the trees sway to and fro.

So fill your cup with woodland zest,
In this odd place, we are our best.
With each warm sip, our spirits free,
Mystic teas bring folks in glee!

## Secrets of the Windy Hollow

In the hollow where breezes play,
Whispers giggle, come what may.
A secret told, a secret shared,
In this place, no one is scared.

The trees conspire, leaves in jest,
While winds weave tales, they know us best.
A squirrel sneezes—oh how it rolls!
And laughter echoes through our souls.

With every gust, a prank in store,
Tickling toes or slamming doors!
The shadows chase, the sun holds strong,
In this hollow, we all belong.

So sit awhile, let worries fade,
Embrace the joy that nature made.
With every wind that lifts your heart,
In windy hollow, we play our part.

www.ingramcontent.com/pod-product-compliance
Lightning Source LLC
Chambersburg PA
CBHW071817160426
43209CB00003B/126